The Body Builder

Charles Carrington

Text copyright © Charles Carrington 1998
Illustrations, Mike Carter
Cover design, David Andrassy
Back cover photograph, Stella Fitzpatrick
Editor, Stella Fitzpatrick
First published & distributed by Gatehouse Books Ltd in 1998
Reprinted 2000 by Gatehouse Books Ltd
Hulme Adult Education Centre, Stretford Road, Manchester M15 5FQ
Printed by RAP Ltd., Rochdale.
ISBN 0 906253 58 6
British Library cataloguing in publication data:
A catalogue record for this book is available from the British Library

Two Gatehouse Book Selection Groups recommended this story for publication.
Many thanks for their work to Nora Ashton, Irene Leech, Mary Morris and Josie
Roche at Newton House & Sandra Brown, Beverley Chadderton, Christine Jones,
Gail Rocca, John Smith, Kevin Summers and Hugh Walsh at Spurley Hey Centre

Thanks also to basic skills groups run by Manchester Adult Education Services at
The Birtles, Greenheys, Newton House, Plant Hill and Varna Centres and to Moya
Curran's group in Stockport with whom we piloted a first draft of this book

Gatehouse also acknowledges continued financial support from Manchester City
Council and North West Arts Board

Gatehouse is a member of the Federation of Worker Writers & Community Publishers.

Gatehouse provides an opportunity for writers to express their thoughts and feelings
on aspects of their lives.
The views expressed are not necessarily those of Gatehouse.

Introduction

I only went to school for three days in my life.
I started to learn to read and write 22 years ago.
I went to a boys' club.
It was someone who was in charge of the club
who helped me to learn.
We called him Woody. He was a schoolteacher.

I saw Woody on his own at the club.
I did not want the others to know.
I told him I could not read.
I used to spend time with him in his office.
That is how I learned to read.

Then he told me about a place where I could go
to learn to read and write more.
He did not have the time to teach me.
It was a class in a local library.
I did not know it was there.
It was not very far from where I lived.

Now I would like to tell you another story from my life.
I hope you enjoy it.

Charles Carrington

I would like to thank Barbara my tutor, for sending my
writing to Gatehouse, otherwise my story would have
never been told.

There was this lad at school
called Billy Hall.
He was a bully.
When I was nine years old,
he made my life a misery.

He was older
and in a different class from me.
At playtime he would pick on me
and do things like
make me walk in puddles of water,
so that my shoes and socks
would be wet all day.

I was not very strong as a child.

I was often ill

and had double pneumonia

when I was about four.

I was off school a lot because I was ill.

When you are weak,

the other lads pick on you,

lads like Billy Hall.

And in those days
I could not read and write, you see.
It made life hard.
When you cannot read and write
as a kid
the other lads will say,
"Do not bother with him, he is a dunce."

So, I have always been on my own,

a loner,

keeping myself to myself.

When you are young

and you are bullied

you get that way

that you do not trust people any more.

You grow up with that feeling.

One day, when walking along the road,
I saw a magazine in the newsagents
called *Health and Fitness*.
It cost one and threepence*.
I had one and threepence in my pocket.
I was in luck.

*One and threepence is the same as six pence today.

After that, I saved my pocket money
and bought the magazine every week.
It had lots of pictures of strong men.

My father gave me birthday money
and I bought chest expanders
and began to exercise.
Today, you would use weights
to exercise
but I could not afford to buy weights
out of my pocket money.

Soon, I began to feel fitter.

I was fourteen at this time.

Later on, when I was fifteen,

my father bought me some weights.

THE LEARNING CENTRE
TOWER HAMLETS COLLEGE
POPLAR CENTRE
POPLAR HIGH STREET
LONDON E14 0AF

Then I met a boy called Robin Curry,
who went to a boys' club
not far from where I lived.
He told me that they had
a weight training class
and I could join if I wanted to.
A week later, he called at my house
and took me to the class.

The teacher was called Mr Morley.

He wasn't very tall

but he was very strong.

He was a nice chap.

He told me all about weight training.

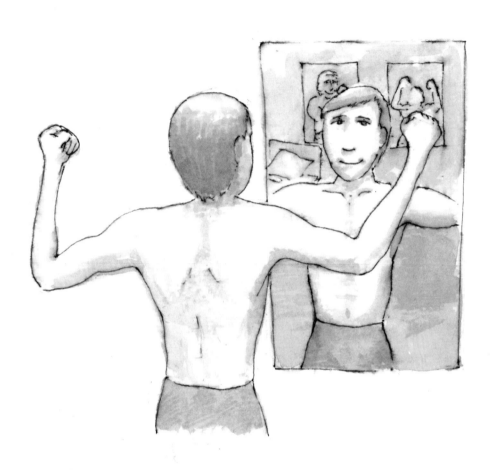

I went three times a week
and I never missed.
I felt a lot stronger and fitter.
At sixteen, I had a forty three inch chest
and my upper arms were fifteen inches.

Years later, I saw Billy Hall.

He was shorter and lighter than me.

In a way, I was glad

that he had bullied me at school,

because it helped me to change my life.

I still do weight training to this day.
I go to classes three times a week.

I am still a loner. I have got used to it.
I like my own company.
I go to reading and writing classes
twice a week. I am now a lot better
at reading and writing than I used to be.

THE LIBRARY
TOWER HAMLETS COLLEGE
POPLAR HIGH STREET
LONDON E14 0AF
Tel: 0207 510 7763

Gatehouse Books

Gatehouse is a unique publisher

Our writers are adults who are developing their basic reading and writing skills. Their ideas and experiences make fascinating material for any reader, but are particularly relevant for adults working on their reading and writing skills. The writing strikes a chord - a shared experience of struggling against many odds.

The format of our books is clear and uncluttered. The language is familiar and the text is often line-broken, so that each line ends at a natural pause.

Gatehouse books are both popular and respected within Adult Basic Education throughout the English speaking world. They are also a valuable resource within secondary schools, Social Services and within the Prison Education Service and Probation Services.

Booklist available

Gatehouse Books
Hulme Adult Education Centre
Stretford Road
Manchester
M15 5FQ
Tel/Fax: 0161 226 7152
E-mail: office@gatehousebooks.org.uk
Website: www.gatehousebooks.org.uk

The Gatehouse Publishing Charity Ltd is a registered charity, no. 1011042
Gatehouse Books Ltd is a company limited by guarantee, reg no. 2619614